# The Bus

# Discriminatory Practice

Shelly Newstead

# The Buskers Guide to Anti-Discriminatory Practice

ISBN - 978-1-904792-23-9
© Shelly Newstead 2006

Illustrations © Chris Bennett 2006

Published by
Common Threads Publications Ltd.
Wessex House
Upper Market Street
Eastleigh
Hampshire SO50 9FD

T: 07000 785215
E: info@commonthreads.org.uk
www.commonthreads.org.uk

**Other titles in The Buskers Guide series include;**
The Buskers Guide to Playwork
The Buskers Guide to Behaviour
The Buskers Guide to Inclusion
The Buskers Guide to Playing Out

The text of 'The Buskers Guide' series can be made available in 14 point font – please contact the publishers by telephoning 07000 785215 or emailing info@commonthreads.org.uk .

# The Buskers Guide to Anti-Discriminatory Practice

## Contents

**Introduction** **page 2**

Chapter 1    **Word Salad**    **page 11**

Chapter 2    **My adp**    **page 33**

Chapter 3    **A hole lot of trouble . . .**    **page 51**

Chapter 4    **page 63**

# Introduction

One of my many and varied 'pre-play' jobs was being a Development Education Worker for Oxfam. My role was to go into schools to work with children and teachers to encourage some balance about developing world issues in the curriculum. At that time there was an awful lot of television coverage about Africa in particular, but it was all desperately negative – famines, wars, disease, and lots of fundraising appeals with pictures of starving children. Children were being taught all about the problems of Africa and, of course, encouraged to fundraise to help the starving, but very little else. Africa was being portrayed as a place where only bad things happened and where nobody could do anything about it – least of all, the people themselves. Children were therefore being bombarded with stereotypical images of black people in Africa who were destitute, helpless and needed our pity.

I have very fond memories of going to primary schools, standing in front of assemblies of 200 children and showing slides of Nairobi, a bustling city with people going to work along busy main roads. The children were hardly able to contain themselves. Without waiting for my questions about what they could see in the pictures, they bounced up and down on the floor, hands waving frenetically, calling out breathlessly, 'But miss – *miss*! They've got cars – and streetlights – and … he's wearing a *suit*!!!' The pictures they were seeing simply didn't match up to those stereotypical images they'd formed in their heads as a result of what they'd been taught or had heard about people in Africa – and, children being children, they wanted to know the reasons why.

Well, thank goodness, that was a long time ago and how times have changed. Or have they? Well, it could be argued that we're generally a lot more aware of developing world issues and that there is less stereotypical coverage. Children now get taught about fair trade in school, for example, and see pictures of people in Africa working hard to supply them with some of their daily luxuries. Media coverage is by and large more balanced nowadays, with the national overseas aid charities having got to grips with the fact that stereotypical images of poverty and misery may help to get the cash in in the short-term, but long-term development can only really take place when peoples' hearts and minds are pushing for change in the way that the world works. Stereotypical images to encourage sympathy, out – images of people going about their daily business to encourage empathy, in. Children also nowadays of course have the great 'www' and can access for themselves a range of non-stereotypical images and music from all around the world at a touch of a button.

So the world of stereotypes and stereotypical thinking around the children that we work with has shifted in the last twenty years, making it easier in many ways to think about people rather than problems. But what about us professionals working with children – how are we doing when it comes to contributing to this shift? Not only to the understanding of children in the area of developing world issues, but to their general understanding of diversity and equality both at home and abroad?

Well, I think we've still got some way to go. And the reason for this? Well, because of the answer to two very different questions I'm afraid. How are we contributing to children's understanding and appreciation of diversity and equality? We 'do anti-discriminatory practice'. Why have we still got some way to go in helping children to truly understand and appreciate diversity and equality? Because we 'do anti-discriminatory practice'.

Now don't get me wrong, I really do believe that the vast majority of us are trying very hard to get it right –

but in some cases I think it could be argued that we are trying too hard. We seem to have gone from one extreme to another in the last twenty years. From not really realising that children with physical impairments can take part in most, if not all activities, to now practically insisting in some settings that all children have to be able to do everything if it's to happen at all. From neither really knowing nor minding about Farid's religious needs and giving him a ham sandwich for his lunch just like all the other kids, to asking his parents to come in and explain their 'funny food habits' to all the children as an 'educational activity'. From being grateful that the boys are happy playing football day in, day out, to making sure that every time they want to play football they take a couple of girls out to play with them too - whether the girls like it or not.

It's not that we're not trying, and it's not that most of us aren't incredibly well-intentioned. And in the vast majority of settings it's certainly not the case that we're not 'doing' enough. But the trouble with 'doing anti-discriminatory practice' is that if we're not very careful, we forget to pay attention to *why* we're doing all the trying and the doing.

Because the danger with all the trying, the worrying about trying, and the 'doing' is that it breeds fear. Fear about not getting it right, fear of offending someone, fear of being seen to get it wrong, fear of being accused of being some sort of unacceptable '-ist', etc etc. And the fear stops us thinking – it stops us paying attention to what we're actually trying to achieve, it stops us questioning the logic of what we're actually 'doing'. Training courses and books and helpful leaflets from helpful agencies that give us short answers to a long question - how do we put anti-discriminatory practice into practice? – only serve to compound our fear and worry – because if we're not doing X, or we haven't got Y, then we must be doing it wrong – help!

So we push on with the doing and the trying, for fear of not being seen to do or try. And while we're very busy with all that effort and action, we simply forget to pay attention – to what anti-discriminatory practice actually means, to the real needs of children and families. We get caught up in labels, checklists, policies, and the perceived 'needs' that we think their label generates. We lose sight of who people really are and go into a flat spin of *doing* things to 'welcome' them, rather than *being* with them (and ourselves) to make sure that we've listened, heard and shared. We hope that all our 'doing' will show off our good (anti-discriminatory practice) intentions, when in fact all it really does is rob us of the time and the energy to pay attention to others and ourselves. Time, energy and attention that could be far better focussed on people than on wondering about the best place to stick the 'welcome' poster.

The problem with the tick-box mentality and the 'equal opps equipment' is that it sort of misses the point. Ok, let's be honest about this – it doesn't *sort of* miss the point at all, it actually wouldn't recognise the point if it jumped up on a table, took all it's clothes off and shouted, 'I'm the point, get me out of here!' The point being, of course, that anti-discriminatory practice is not a finite project, it's a state of mind. Anti-discriminatory practice ought to be part of the way that we all think, feel, act and react when we work with children, not as something 'special' or 'extra' to the way that we already work. It is a process which should come as naturally to our everyday practice as talking to children about their day or washing our hands before preparing food. And just like all the other parts of our professional practice, it is a process on which we need to reflect.

For many people who work with children, anti-discriminatory practice is second nature – not only is it part of their day-to-day good practice, it seems to just be part of who they are. But even for some of these people, what appears to be common sense in the way that they treat other human beings gets clouded in the particular (and even peculiar) fashions of the day – different models, jargon and terminology, the newest equipment 'must-haves' or the latest bright idea from a training course. It can be hard in the face of the 'finite project' model to keep the thinking processes clear and open and to resist the temptation to be in with the in-crowd – because, apart from any other reason, nobody wants to be seen to be 'discriminatory'.

So we need to look at this whole anti-discriminatory practice thing in a different way. Let's re-visit what we are trying to achieve in the name of anti-discriminatory practice and pause for a while on the roller-coaster of expensive 'multi-cultural equipment', meaningless equal opportunities polices and 'celebrating' Diwali in the baby room in nurseries (no, really – it happens). Before we rush off to 'do' anti-discriminatory practice, we need to be clear on what anti-discriminatory practice really means – both for us and, even more importantly, for the children that we work with.

**Shelly Newstead**

**PS** – Just before you get started - anti-discriminatory practice is a heck of a long phrase, and as you've probably already noticed, Buskers Guides are pretty small books! Once this book was finished, we worked out that we needed an extra five pages just to be able to keep in the references to the topic of the book! So I hope you won't mind, but anti-discriminatory practice is referred to often throughout the book as adp. Technically speaking of course this is a grammatical crime, but not only has it helped to keep it within normal page length but it should also make it easier to read – hope it works for you!

**PPS** – Sorry, nearly forgot – we really like to hear from our Buskers Guide readers – apart from anything else, you're such an interesting bunch! Please send your feedback on this Buskers Guide (or anything else for that matter, including ideas for future Buskers Guides perhaps?!) to buskersguides@commonthreads.co.uk.

# Chapter 1
# Word salad

I guess it won't come as a surprise to anybody who works with children to hear that anti-discriminatory practice is an essential part of our work. The phrase turns up everywhere – in legal requirements, quality assurance schemes, national occupational standards… It doesn't matter where you work with children or at what level, we all need to 'do' anti-discriminatory practice.

But before we can 'do' anything about adp, we first of all need to get to grips with some of the language which gets served up in that rather exotic, but somehow pretty indigestible, adp word salad. We might all agree that the words and phrases which we find in policies, documents and booklets are good things, ought to be there, should be done (or not, as the case may be)… but when it comes down to brass tacks, what is it that we actually should be doing?

## Diversity

When it comes to adp, the word 'diversity' often gets interpreted as meaning 'different people', or, even more dubious, 'people who are different to me'. This leads us straight into murky waters, because we then start thinking about 'different groups of people' – vegetarians, people with disabilities, refugees, the people who live on that estate, etc. We start to think about their 'diverse needs' and try to make sure that we are doing things to include people from these 'groups'.

Yet if we think about this logically, we all have diverse needs – because diversity actually just means variety, different kinds – as in, human beings are a diverse lot. It sounds really trite to say 'we are all different' – but we are. So lumping lots of different, individual people together (just because they are 'different' or 'different to me') and applying a label to them is a bit daft really when you to come to think about it – especially when it's done in the name of anti-discriminatory practice!

Because let's face it, even if some people do feel that they want to identify themselves as part of a 'group', this doesn't mean that they all share every characteristic or that the group label is the only thing that is of any relevance or interest about them. If this were the case, then the meetings of the 'right-handed, short-sighted, white single hetero-sexual

People who are exactly like me Group meeting

men who are (nearly) aged 45, concerned about going slightly bald, hate football and would prefer tea to coffee any time' group would be very dull indeed (not to say difficult to fit on headed paper!).

And while we're on the topic I just need to add that I always get rather worried when I hear people talking about 'the… community' – as in 'the gay community' or 'the Jewish community'. I worry because it really does sound like the person speaking believes that all the people with that particular label are all living together as one big happy family – presumably in tents somewhere on a very, very large field. And if that's not the case, then what on earth is 'the black community'? Can you image somebody turning up on the news as 'Gladys, a spokesperson from the white community'? Which community – and why is Gladys able to speak for all of them anyway? Do they all really think like her – I would very much doubt it! This way of speaking seems to be used to refer the audience that 'the people I am talking about are a bit different and their views might be a bit different to yours – stand by your beds!' Another word that gets similarly misused is 'race' – there is actually only one human race, so referring to someone as being from a 'different race' presumably means that they are from the planet Zog!

It is of course just a little ironic that a word such as 'diversity' can get applied in a way which turns out to mean the exact opposite. We hear a lot about 'valuing individuals' in our line of work, but what often gets missed is that what we're actually talking about is all individuals, everybody, the whole diverse lot of us (not 'them'!) – even the ones we don't like/don't understand/can't get on with – and especially those who are just so individual that no label gets anywhere close! Welcoming diversity means exactly that – understanding that everybody is different to everybody else, even if they live in the same street, are followers of one particular faith, come from the same family, etc.

Of course, everyone is the same underneath – except for those who are different – and some people are more different than others.

So before we go any further, if your setting does have one of *those* policies – you know the ones, they start off with something like, 'We will be nice to everybody – regardless of whether they are….', please go and shred it now. Because when you think about it, it is a little bizarre that in a (well-meaning) effort to show that we are trying to 'cater for' diversity in our setting, we make a list of groups of people that we are going to pay attention to. I hope you'll agree that, however long your list, you are always going to miss someone out. Those lists are usually very clear about the need not to discriminate against disabled people, for example – but what about single dads who are transvestites? And if your skin is not white, you're probably at least covered by the list, but what about if you're old – and Polish – and speak with a lisp? What is it that are we really trying to say here – that there are some 'groups' that we are nicer to than others? Don't know about you, but that doesn't sound very much like welcoming diversity to me!

So getting to grips with this seemingly innocent little word, 'diversity', takes us a long way towards understanding what adp is not – it's not about looking at 'groups' of people and working out how 'they' can be included in the setting, because those groups as we perceive them don't actually exist. But before we get ahead of ourselves, a few more tasty morsels from our word salad…

## Equal opportunities

Tricky one, this. Equal opportunities often gets confused with anti-discriminatory practice as being one and the same thing – but you'll probably not be surprised to hear that it isn't.

We can say that anti-discriminatory practice is part of equal opportunities, if that helps at all to start with. But anti-discriminatory practice is what individual practitioners do, and equal opportunities is what an organisation does. In other words, equal opportunities is about ensuring that everything that your setting does, from the way it recruits people, to the physical layout of a room, to the way that it deals with health and safety issues, is done in a way which means that demonstrates that diversity is seen as a good thing in your setting and that all the relevant legal requirements are met.

To offer real equality of opportunity means that we need to think outside of our own experiences, our own values and our own attitudes to evaluate and sometimes change the way that our setting does something – and this is where anti-discriminatory practice comes in. It's not possible to have equality of opportunity without adp, but we can have adp without equal opportunities, because anti-discriminatory practice is about our own professional practice and the way that we think and act. The results of adp being applied to ourselves determines the way that we behave. When the results of our personal reflection is

applied to our setting and becomes part of our settings'
policies and procedures, it becomes 'equal
opportunities'.

Not sure if that bit was a bit tough – if so, please feel
free to go back and have another chew!

## 'Non-judgemental'

People often say anti-discriminatory practice is about
being non-judgemental. But in our profession, I hope
you'll agree it is actually very important to make
judgements and to be able to do this in a professional
way for the benefit and protection of the children we
work with.

Anti-discriminatory practice doesn't require us to give
up making *professional* judgements – it just requires us
not to apply or impose our *personal* values and attitudes
to the children and families we work with. In other
words, making assumptions about children just because
they come from a particular family (because that family
is 'different to other families in the setting') is not ok,
but making a judgement about a child who is being hurt
or harmed in some way on the basis of professional
concern is a requirement of our role.

So an important part of anti-discriminatory practice is
distinguishing between our own personal values and

attitudes and our professional responsibilities and then making sure that it is our professional values we are acting on, rather than our personal ones.

## 'Political correctness'

Now I just need to share something with you at this point – I really loathe this phrase. It just makes my hackles rise – usually because it seems to imply that the reason that anti-discriminatory practice exists is just to keep people (or even worse, 'them', whoever 'they' might be) happy, or that we say or do certain things that 'should' be said or done just for the sake of being more 'right on' than the next person, because it's simply the thing to do.

So here goes – political correctness does not, and should not, exist in our field. Why not? Because discrimination can harm children's development and their potential and that's the reason that anti-discriminatory practice is a professional requirement.

'Nuff said - moving on.

## Discrimination

Phew, I think we got over the 'p.c.' bit pretty quickly! Now we need to get to grips with this discrimination thing – because, in the words of the song, whatever it is, we're against it...!

Believe everything you hear and discrimination appears to be happening to everybody roughly every five minutes. People often joke on training courses that they have been 'discriminated against' because they are the only one in the group who hasn't got a handout. Children in a school dinner hall say it's discrimination when they

I DON'T LIKE TO BE ANTI-ANYTHING - SO I'M PRO-ANTI-DISCRIMINATORY PRACTICE

are told that they can't have second helpings because children on the other table have finished it all up. Members of staff in a setting whinge that 'discrimination' is taking place when they are asked to stay behind after work to sort out the equipment cupboard.

Interesting word, discrimination… but often not used in the right way.

Because this discrimination that we're against is not about people being treated unfairly, being left out, or even treated differently. Discrimination in the context of anti-discriminatory practice has a very specific meaning, which is: discrimination is unfair treatment based on prejudice.

Unfair treatment, yes – but the bit that makes the difference as to whether it's discrimination or not is the last bit – discrimination is unfair treatment *based on prejudice*. Enter another tricky word – and one that also often gets used out of context!

## Prejudice

A prejudice is simply a false belief – or in other words and in the context of adp, something that we think, or assume, about people which is not based on complete facts. Some things that we believe may of course be based on 'the truth' – but a version of 'the truth' only as we know or have experienced it.

For example, it may be entirely true that a child who came to your setting last year who was blind needed one-to-one support. But if we took that one experience and assumed it to be true of all children who are blind, then we would end up with the false belief that all children who are blind need one-to-one support. If we then applied this false belief to the next blind child who turned up at our setting (for example, by arranging for somebody to be with her at all times), without first of all checking out the 'facts' as they applied to this particular blind child, (ie, does she actually need someone to be with her at all times) then we would

probably end up treating her unfairly on the basis of our prejudice. In other words, we would be discriminating against her – despite the fact that the way we behaved

22

towards this child might have started with the best of intentions.

While we're here and thinking about the best of intentions, let's just fish out of our word salad the phrase 'positive discrimination'. Sometimes this is the phrase which gets used to mean, 'Well, we did discriminate, but we did it for good reasons, so it doesn't really count.' This is another case of getting our meanings in a muddle. Discrimination is the unfair treatment of people based on prejudice – so whatever the motive, if prejudice is the cause of the unfair treatment, it's discrimination.

As uncomfortable as it might be to admit, if our child who is blind doesn't need one-to-one support, but we make the false assumption that she does and act on that assumption, then we are in danger of limiting the development of her independence skills. By providing close supervision at all times, we could be depriving that child of the opportunity to develop in the same way that all children develop – by trying out new things, learning from their successes and their failures, finding out how to take risks in a way that she is comfortable with and getting to know when to ask for help from others. We could also be undermining her confidence, in that the independence she has gained is taken away from her and she loses the confidence to try out independence skills in the future. So however well-meaning we were to start with, by treating her unfairly according to our prejudices, we will be harming her development.

But how do we tell the difference between discrimination and different treatment, I hear you cry? Surely it's not ok to treat everybody the same – but how do we know when we're treating people differently so that their needs are met, rather than acting on the basis of prejudice?

Good question – and there you also have the answer to what anti-discriminatory practice is all about. It is about being reflective about our own thoughts and processes to find out whether our false beliefs are getting the better of us and getting in the way of our professional practice – and if they are, then adapting our behaviour accordingly. Not an easy answer to the question I'm afraid, but at least we've got a grip on what adp is now if that's any comfort!

Prejudice? Not in here, there isn't

(By the way, positive

discrimination is a phrase which is used to mean something very specific in employment law – but that's equal opportunities and far beyond the scope of this Buskers Guide I'm afraid, so we're just going to have to leave that one in our salad bowl, sorry!)

## Stereotypes

Trainspotting

There are an awful lot of stereotypes – and they can cause an awful lot of mirth! I could probably fill the rest of this book with one long list of stereotypes without even having to think very hard at all. We all know them... Germans (deck chair hoggers), male hairdressers (gay), women drivers (unpredictable), trainspotters (male nerds), football fans (hooligans), Essex girls (fill in your own brackets…!) and on they go. Stereotypes turn up everywhere – in the newspapers, in jokes, in adverts (how many adverts for washing powder have you seen where it's men getting ecstatic about the whiteness of their whites?!) – they are part of our day-to-day lives.

We also of course are more than capable of creating our own stereotypes. Remember earlier in this chapter that we were thinking about not applying labels to 'groups' of people just because they have a few things in common? Well, this is what I call 'groupthink', and the trouble with groupthink is that it gives rise to stereotypical thinking.

We can think of any stereotype as an image or a label about people which we carry around in our heads. Sometimes we know they're there – and sometimes we don't. Just for a bit of light relief at this point, try the exercise on the page opposite. All you need to do is draw in the boxes the first image that comes to mind when you read the word – have fun!

So, what sort of pictures did you get? Many people get images which, although just actually being the word which means 'the male/female version of', actually give out very different messages. For example, 'bachelors' are often fun-loving, young party animals whilst 'spinsters' often turn out as older, lonely ladies – sometimes even with a spinning wheel!

| | |
|---|---|
| Landlord | Landlady |
| Master | Mistress |
| Bachelor | Spinster |
| Wizard | Witch |

Of course, not everybody comes up with these images and whether you did or not doesn't mean that you are any more or less prone to think in stereotypes than anybody else. But two things always interest me when I do that sort of exercise on training courses. First of all, lots of people come up with those same images. And secondly, many people will say that they know that widows can be young/bachelors can be lonely and are therefore worried about why their immediate reaction was exactly the opposite!

Many of us do have images in our heads that may or may not represent the way we actually think – but

nonetheless they are there. We all need to pay a great deal of attention to these images and the potential for such stereotypes to exist in our heads, so that they don't catch us unawares. Because one of the awkward things about stereotypes is that they can affect how we think without us realising it…

## S-P-D

So discrimination happens when people are treated unfairly because of prejudices (false beliefs) held about them and prejudices can be formed from stereotypes – the image or the label that we assign to people.

So not getting a handout on a training course is not, of course, discrimination, it's just an oversight – unless, that is, the trainer thinks that you have been quiet all morning and therefore must be a bit dim, so hasn't bothered to give you a handout because he has assumed you obviously won't be able to read it (**s**tereotype = quiet, **p**rejudice = less than bright, **d**iscrimination = no handout). And not getting seconds in the dinner hall is just unlucky, maybe it will be your turn next time – unless, of course, the dinner lady has taken a look at your nice clean and tidy uniform and decided that you obviously don't need seconds because you must get very well fed at home (**s**tereotype = well-off, **p**rejudice =

well cared for at home, **d**iscrimination = no second helpings).

The bad news here is, of course, that stereotypes can easily lead to prejudices, which in turn can easily lead to discrimination. But there is good news too – and that is that if we are aware of this process, we can stop it in it's tracks so that it doesn't lead to discrimination. And there's more good news – we'll be looking at how to do this in Chapter 2!

## Anti-discriminatory practice

But before we get there, we'll just linger over our last mouthful of word salad. Anti-discriminatory practice is about being against discrimination (no surprises, no prizes!) – and discrimination is about the different treatment of people based on prejudice. Prejudice is something very personal to us, because we all have false beliefs which are based on partial truth, misunderstandings, and stereotypes. So anti-discriminatory practice is also something which is very personal to us – part of our individual professional practice which helps us to ensure that our own values and attitudes, important and invaluable as they are to us, do not have a negative impact on the children and families we work with. Adp is also of course about ensuring that other peoples' values and attitudes do not have a negative effect on people in our setting and we will look at this in Chapter 4.

So anti-discriminatory practice is not simply about focussing on the 'usual suspects' of skin colour, creed or dis/ability (or in other words, those 'groups' that appear in those ghastly lists). Neither is it something that we do to make sure that we are 'being nice to people who are different to us', or even to satisfy those pesky external requirements. Instead it is something that we need to put into practice constantly as professionals who want the very best for the children we work with.

Of course making sure that we don't discriminate against people because of their skin colour, creed or dis/abilty is important – but it's also important to remember that just about everybody has the potential to be treated differently on the basis of prejudice, regardless of whether they fall into one of those (or any other) 'groups' or not. Adp is therefore not just about 'minorities', or 'groups', or 'special needs', it is about everybody and how we relate to each other.

So now if we've all finished our salad it's time to stop eating our words and get on with this adp thing instead!

Guess the odd one out...

George    Bill    Stan    Graham    Eddie

Yes, Stan hasn't got his level 3 yet!

# Chapter 2
# My Adp

We said in Chapter 1 that anti-discriminatory practice is part of our individual professional practice, about how we act and react to *all* the children and adults we work with. So in this chapter we are going to look at what we need to do to put anti-discriminatory practice into... well, practice! Or more specifically, how we are going to put adp into *our* practice.

## Spot the S-P-D

Very few of us can claim to be all-knowing – and we'd probably be pretty unbearable if we could! So isn't it only natural that we make a few assumptions to help us along when faced by a similar situation next time?

*I don't make assumptions, and I can tell just by looking at you that you don't either.*

Of course it is – natural and very common. None of us knows everything, so we throw in a few assumptions every now and again to fill in the gaps, using past experience and knowledge - either our own, or knowledge and experience which originally belonged to other people. Sometimes we get lucky and our assumptions turn out to be correct. Sometimes they're not right – but if we hang on to them anyway, that's when they turn into prejudices. So before we allow those prejudices to influence the way we treat people (ie, discriminate against them), we first of all need to check out whether we are actually working on the basis of fact (as it applies to this particular situation) or false beliefs.

One of the awkward things about stereotypes is that there are of course people who fit the stereotypes. No doubt there are some Germans who do like to be first in the deckchairs, just as there are some people who go to football matches who cause trouble. But then there are also many Italians who enjoy first pick of the deckchairs of a morning and lots of people who go to watch football who only raise their fists once a goal is scored!

So even when we're thinking about a situation that we may have come across before, we need to think critically about whether we are actually working on fact rather than reacting to stereotypes – because as we know, stereotypes can easily give rise to prejudices, and prejudices can lead us to discrimination.

For example, think about the child who is from 'that family', or 'the child who is a refugee'. Is there an image in your head that goes with that phrase when you think about it – and if so, what are the spontaneous thoughts and feelings that spring to mind? Thoughts and feelings can automatically attach themselves to stereotypes – we start to form judgements and opinions about somebody based on the image that we get in our heads. Does the thought of the child from 'that family' start to wind you up, for example, or do you feel sorry for the child who is a refugee?

And now for the acid test – are these thoughts and feelings based on fact, are they actually about the child we are thinking about? Or have those feelings come from a stereotype? The child who is a refugee, for example, might need you to feel sorry for him and help him – but on the other hand he could be having the time of his life. The child from 'that family' might indeed warrant the feelings of trepidation and frustration – but she might actually be a very quiet child who causes no bother whatsoever and is a real joy to be with.

So one of the very first things we need to do when it comes to putting anti-discriminatory practice into our practice is to check our thinking before we act. Are we making assumptions about somebody, are we re-acting to a stereotype rather than the person in front of us, are we using information or experience from the past which may not be applicable to this situation? If so, we need to be honest with ourselves – and maybe others –

so that we can put a spoke in the wheel of stereotype-prejudice-discrimination.

## Honesty

Now this is where it starts to get tough. It should all be downhill from here on in, but let's face it – if we're going to be pro-active and make adp part of our everyday practice, then the place start is with ourselves.

And I think that's it's true to say that this can be difficult. No-body likes to admit they're 'in the wrong', and no-body really wants to admit to having prejudices. We also don't like to think of any harm being done – to children or adults – by something we may have said or done. And whilst these are all perfectly natural and normal feelings, I'm afraid there's just no polite way to say this – we've got to get over it. Because as professionals, we need to act in a way that is going to mean the best outcome for the children and families we work with – even if this involves us feeling a bit awkward about a few things every now and again.

If it helps at all, remember that, as we said earlier, everybody has prejudices. And as we all have them, it's therefore up to all of us to make sure that these prejudices do not turn into discrimination as part of our everyday professional practice. To do this, we need to focus our attention to make sure that our daily practice includes reflection on our thinking and our actions with regard to stereotype-prejudice-discrimination, and we will need to be prepared to ask ourselves some pretty tough questions, such as;

I don't have any prejudices, and people who say that I must have are probably long-haired hippies who listen to whale-song.

- was what I did/what I said in that situation based on fact?
- did I make any assumptions in that situation – and if I did, were these right or not?
- did I feel uncomfortable about this situation (either before or after it happened) – and if so, was it prejudice that was driving my behaviour?

Remember also that one of the purposes of any sort of reflective practice is to help us to learn from our experiences – so the reason for asking yourself such questions is not to make you feel good or bad about yourself, nor is it to try to establish whether you are 'prejudiced' or not (because we know we all are). If we answer such questions as truthfully and as honestly as we can, then we should be able to recognise when a similar situation happens in the future and to put what we have learnt in the past to good use – either by doing what we did last time to avoid discrimination or in making a deliberate effort not to fall into the same traps as we did last time and therefore avoid discrimination.

## Knowledge (1)

In the bad old days of adp training, some of us had the indescribable pleasure of being made to sit though hours of presentations about what 'people from the XYZ community' (remember 'them'?!) ate/didn't eat/wore/did on their holy days etc etc etc – the implication being that if we didn't know as much as the

trainers did by the end of the session, then we obviously weren't cutting it in the adp department.

The trouble is that, ridiculous as it all seems now, those days have left behind them a bit of a legacy – they have made some of us a bit twitchy about knowing things – or not knowing them, as the case may be. It's very easy to worry that;

- we don't know
- we think we know but might not know really
- somebody else will make us feel bad for not knowing
- whatever we know we're scared we might get it wrong if we do anything about it

It's important to recognise that we can't know everything, because otherwise the worry and the fear can just paralyse us into doing nothing for the fear of getting it wrong – and when it comes to adp, this has to be the worst option of all. Ok, we may get it wrong every now and again, we may even on occasion cause somebody genuine offence. But far better to be able to establish an open and honest relationship with someone where you can ask questions and apologise if necessary rather than hiding behind the bookshelves every time they turn up because you don't know what to say to them!

You sometimes hear people in the field of adp say, 'If you don't know, ask.' Sound advice – much better than going to books and the internet but then getting it wrong because you haven't quite understood the finer details. But then there's another reason for asking – and that's because whatever facts you've gleaned on a particular subject, they still don't relate to that particular person.

Take any label that is applied to people, and you'll see how this works – autistic, vegetarian, old age pensioner...We all (hopefully) now understand that autism is a spectrum – so the facts of what this label means to each individual are going to differ. 'Vegetarian' is a word that people seem to use to mean anything from 'doesn't eat meat – but fish is ok' to 'won't wear leather shoes'. And as for old age pensioner... well, what was your mental image – a 67-year old in a care home or an 87 year old parachutist?!

So whilst 'If you don't know, ask', is generally sound advice, I would actually go one step further and suggest instead, 'If you do know, ask.' Two reasons for this – first of all you might get a few surprises, and secondly, even if the other person is confirming what you knew anyway, at least you get a chance to build a relationship with them and to really demonstrate that you're paying attention – to them, rather than to a description of them.

## Knowledge (2)

We've all heard of the phrase 'a little knowledge is a dangerous thing' and this has more than a grain of truth to it when it comes to adp. Because as we saw in Chapter 1, applying our knowledge of one person to another could lead us into thinking in stereotypes (and we all know where that leads us!).

We need to make sure that our knowledge, regardless

of what amount of it we have and on what subject, is relevant to the person that we are working with. Jo Bloggs might come from the same family as Jim Bloggs, but the knowledge that you have about Jo isn't going to help you much when trying to figure out how to relate to Jim. And if it's two people we are dealing with who happen to have the same label, then we need to make sure that we are treating them as individuals, rather than according to their label. After all, if we know not to treat two girls from Dundee who are aged seven the same (just because they both happen to be girls and both aged seven), then why should two girls from Somalia be like each other?

Finding ourselves having to deal with new situations can sometimes drive us to think that we are in some way lacking – that we just don't know how to cope because we haven't got enough/the right/specialist knowledge. And then we forget that all we are doing is dealing with is people – maybe they have different accents, maybe they look physically different to you, maybe they get around differently – but they're still just people, after all. So instead of trying to grasp for what little bits of knowledge that may have come in useful in a different situation, we simply need to accept that this is going to probably be worse than useless, and enjoy the challenge of getting to know some new people!

# Knowledge (3)

There may, of course, be some knowledge that instinctively we feel that we would rather not have. We might not want to know more about how some people live their lives, or there may be things that we know about some people but really we'd rather not. We're not talking here about stuff that's illegal or harmful to children, of course, because as we said in Chapter 1 in those circumstances we all know what we need to do with that knowledge. But what we are talking about is the small details of how some people think and behave that just make us feel – well, uncomfortable, because some things clash with our own personal values and attitudes.

If we are going to avoid discrimination in this instance, we need to make sure that we do know what we think we know, and that we're not just reacting to gossip, assumptions or stereotypes. If what is making us feel uncomfortable is the way that people look or the way that we think that they behave according to their label, then we are being made to feel uncomfortable by a stereotype, not by the person themselves. In other words, we need to make sure that we are not acting on prejudices (false beliefs), and what we feel uncomfortable about is actually true about the individual person we are dealing with.

And if it really is the person that we know who is

making us feel uncomfortable (rather than the stereotypical image of them), then we need to make sure that our behaviour towards them still demonstrates our professional values rather than our personal ones.

## Language

Sometimes you hear people say that language changes. But when you think about it, it doesn't actually – the words stay the same, it's just that what people understand by those words changes.

It's the understanding and the thinking behind language that changes, and that's why the whole subject of 'language' when it comes to adp is a very tricky one. Because not only does understanding change over time, it also changes differently for individuals – one person's idea of what is the most appropriate language will differ from another person's. Language doesn't change because of 'political correctness' (see Chapter 1 if you missed my small rant on that subject!), it changes because we are all different and understanding and interpretation of words and their meanings changes as people change.

Or to put it another way, one man might think that it's perfectly acceptable to refer to somebody who is female as a 'lady', whilst the next man may have strong views that the word 'woman' is more appropriate. Put them in a room with two females, one of whom is definitely not going to be called a 'lady' by anyone (because she feels patronised by the word) and the other one who doesn't give two hoots what she is called as long as it's not rude, and hopefully you can see nub of the great language dilemma!

There are of course some words which are generally considered to be out-of-date, offensive, and/or no longer accurate. However, I'm not going to list them here, because apart from the obvious reason of not wanting to cause any offence, neither do I want you falling off your chair with laughter if you are reading this book ten years after it was first written! Rather than trying to learn the 'latest way of saying things' and then still getting it 'wrong' when it comes to how one individual uses certain words, we need to adopt a more laid-back approach to the whole language issue. If we are open and honest in our professional practice, then we can accept that we might not always get language 'right', and easily change our language use if what we say could cause offence.

There are several things we can do other than having to wait to see if our language use is going to offend anybody. We can think about the words from the other person's point of view and to try to think how we would feel if we were being described in that way. We can also ask ourselves whether we need to refer to anybody by any language other than their name? And if it is absolutely necessary, can we use the language that the person

So what's your name — er, that is er, Christian — I mean first — you know, you might not be er christian, I mean, I'm not — well, I don't think so — er, you don't look er, you know, foreign — but that doesn't mean — you know — I'll try to pronounce it correctly — shall we write it down — I'm not assuming you can write...

P.C. Terms

They call me Fred at School.

themselves prefer — and the best way to find that out is, of course, to ask them!

The other thing that we can do when thinking about the appropriateness of specific words or phrases is to try to find out where they come from — do they have any negative or positive connotations associated with them? In other words, if we approach the language issue with the same professional values and standards as we apply to everything else we do, the whole thing becomes a much less daunting topic.

## 'Being' adp

So at the end of this chapter hopefully you will understand where I'm coming from when I say that putting anti-discriminatory practice into our practice isn't so much about 'doing' adp but about 'being' adp. Or to put it another way, we can put up as many 'welcome' posters as we have wall space in our settings, but if we are thinking, feeling and doing things that make other people feel uncomfortable about who they are, then all that blue-tak simply goes to waste.

Because anti-discriminatory practice is about being self-aware, being a reflective practitioner and, most of all, being honest about what we think, feel and know. Being 'against discrimination' means that we have to be open to the fact that we might have to deal with stereotypes, prejudice and discrimination in ourselves as well as others and to be able to do this as part of our normal, everyday practice.

And once we've got this adp, this way of thinking, acting and re-acting, into our everyday practice, then it shouldn't feel like we're 'doing' anything at all – it's just the way things happen in our settings. Stereotypes are moved on, prejudices are tested and discrimination becomes a thing of the past – right? Ah yes, except for one thing….

…our settings. Full steam ahead to Chapter 3 – but do mind the black hole as you turn the page!

# Chapter 3
# **A hole lot of trouble...**

So we've done the hard bit – we've looked at our own thoughts, been really honest, even perhaps been brave enough to admit to the odd stereotype and false belief here and there... so great, well done, now time to relax? Ah, sorry, no – not quite.

You see, we haven't faced the black hole of discrimination yet. I know we said in Chapter 1 that adp is about personal practice and that equal opportunities is about practical stuff in your setting, and you'll be glad to hear that I haven't changed my mind on you at the start of Chapter 3! However, some of the things that get done in the name of equal opportunities can actually work against what we're trying to do in the name of anti-discriminatory practice – and that's where the black hole starts to beckon.

Because believe it or not (and I do hope that it's not a 'not' by the end of this chapter!), some of the things we put into place in our settings can actually create stereotypes – not only in our minds but also in the minds of the children we work with. And we all know from Chapter 1 where stereotypes can lead us... So if that isn't too scary, perhaps you'd like to come a bit closer to the edge of the black hole and take a closer look.....

## Equipment

Anybody surprised by what you saw going into the black hole of discrimination at the start of the chapter? Anybody wondering why some of those things are going in – when actually you might have thought that they were the very things to keep discrimination at bay?

Well, the short answer is that in trying to represent 'diversity', what we can actually end up doing is creating and perpetuating stereotypes. For example, people often tell me that the whole purpose of a 'multi-cultural home corner' is that we are showing children that 'different people have different ways of cooking.' But hang on a minute – 'different people'? Doesn't that sound a bit like groupthink? Which 'different people' – is it Chinese people we are talking about here? In which case are we sure that that's all Chinese people cook with, before we start to reinforce such dodgy stereotypes? And I don't know about you, but I'm a dab hand with a wok – and just for the record, I was born in Norfolk! Perhaps you could argue that people who come from Norfolk are different (but that would be a stereotype so you wouldn't, would you?!), but I don't think we're any more 'different' to anybody else!

And it's not just the multi-cultural home corner equipment that's in danger of propelling us into the black hole of discrimination, it's all the whole panoply of stuff that gets sold in the name of 'celebrating diversity' – the dressing up clothes, musical instruments, dolls etc etc. The difficulty with all this stuff is that it can create new stereotypes. To portray 'different people' as having 'different habits' is just replacing one set of stereotypes with another. We know of course that Chinese people do not all cook exclusively with woks, that not all African musicians sit under trees playing gourds (African rock has been around for a long time and I bet the kids you work with would find this a darn sight more interesting than scraping a piece of wood!), and many Asian women wear jeans and tee-shirts.

So if – and I have to admit that it's a very big 'if' in my book – we do have some of this 'multi-cultural' equipment in our settings, we have to be very careful how we present it to children. Putting a cardboard label on a gourd saying 'an African instrument' can create (and perhaps even reinforce) stereotypes and prejudices of poverty, lack of technology and lack of technical ability – why not get out an electric guitar and label that as 'an African instrument' instead? Telling children that

'Chinese people cook with woks' is simply not the whole picture – and therefore it's a stereotype.

In our well-meaning intentions of exposing children to the wider world, it is all too easy to fall into the stereotypes and prejudices which inevitably go with the things that are beyond our own experience. Trying to 'represent diversity' in our settings is a bit like trying to 'represent colour' – we could have all our primary colours 'represented' with some nice blues, greens, reds and blacks, but what about all the other colours, and all the shades in between all of those colours? As with people, any 'representation' is going to be, by its very nature, tokenistic and therefore stereotypical – and as we know, that way lies the black hole of discrimination…

## Events

And then there's the events…. you know the sorts of events I mean – French week, Hawaiian evening, Chinese New Year – all things that regularly take place in our settings in order to 'celebrate diversity'. Out

come the berets and garlic bread and cardboard boxes for making models of the Eiffel Tower for French week, the grass skirts and the pineapples on the heads for the Hawaiian evening, and the cardboard boxes (again) to make the dragons for Chinese New Year.

Can you feel the tug of that black hole right now – I sure hope so, or we're going in! Because yes, you got it (phew, saved!) – there's our stereotypes again, with quite a few prejudices thrown in for good measure…The French as garlic-eating beret-wearers, the Hawaiians as people who sing and dance all day wearing garlands of flowers and not a lot else – more one-dimensional portrayals of what people are 'like', rather than an acknowledgement of the fact that everybody is different, regardless of labels (which include nationality!).

And when it comes to festivals – well, there's just no bigger opportunity than 'doing a festival' to dive headlong into that black hole! As an example, let's take my favourite – Chinese New Year. To fully understand Chinese New Year celebrations (and I'm not going to pretend here that I do, because I don't), you have to understand beliefs about ancestry, the Chinese calendar, a whole host of taboos and superstitions, ancient legends, the importance of family and identity, traditional gods, how certain food has special significance during the festival…etc, etc, etc…And what do we see after-school clubs up and down England doing in the name of celebrating Chinese New Year? Making lanterns out of kitchen rolls and dragons out of cardboard boxes.

Not only do such activities grossly under-represent the complexity of such an important festival for so many people, they also give children yet again that one-dimensional view of an imaginary 'group' of people – 'the Chinese'. Chinese New Year is celebrated by people who are not Chinese and there are over 50 ethnic minority groups in China who do not celebrate this festival. Oh, and on December 31$^{st}$ (by the Gregorian calendar), the streets of Hong Kong are filled with Chinese people celebrating *that* New Year as well. Given the complexities of religious festivals we do, I feel, really have to question whether children's knowledge and understanding of the world is in any way enhanced by making things out of junk materials in the name of 'celebrating festivals.'

And even if children's family members come into the setting to talk about their celebrations and festivals, we need to remember that they can only speak from their very personal experience, rather than being a spokesperson for their particular faith – because other people who share the same faith may have different customs and practices associated with that festival. And children should not be asked to explain to the rest of the setting about their beliefs, festivals etc – we wouldn't ask a child with two different coloured eyes to explain what it's like to have one green eye and one blue eye, so why should other children have to explain themselves to the rest of the group?

And a final thought about festivals - you don't hear that much about Ethiopian New Year (Rastafarian celebration) or Ridvan (Ba'hai festival). Now please believe me, I'm really not trying to show off my impressive knowledge of religious festivals here – it took me two minutes to find these, and hundreds more festivals, on the wonderful 'www'. But that's sort of my point, you see – I found hundreds of festivals - there are more religious festivals than there are days of the week. Can we really say that we are 'celebrating diversity' if we do the same three or four every year festivals every year?

# Plan B

So does this mean that we should pay no attention whatsoever to trying to 'represent diversity' in our settings? No of course not – it just means that we have to be a bit more sophisticated about how we go about it. Instead of buying the dolls, the instruments, the Japanese food set (which sort of overlooks the fact that you can buy sushi from supermarkets in Wales nowadays), what we need to do is to make sure that we are demonstrating by our choice of equipment and resources that our settings are for everybody. For example;

- art materials that enable children to represent all skin tones
- left-handed and right handed scissors
- resources which show non-stereotypical images (men ironing, women fire-fighters, athletes with physical impairments, homes that are not always houses with gardens, etc)
- pieces of fabric and material that suggest different techniques
- music – take a look on the great 'www' for artists from Japan who play jazz, from Afghanistan who are percussionists, or woodwind players from Iran

In other words, we need to make sure that we are providing resources and equipment that are non-stereotypical – and then also presenting them in a way which does not create stereotypes. So instead of putting on the 'Afghani percussion music' and telling children that 'this is Afghan music', we need to make sure that we are telling them that this is music which is being played by a musician from Afghanistan – because after all, there are percussion players all over the world.

## Equal – but different

Of course we want children to feel comfortable and happy in our settings. But feeling comfortable and happy doesn't rely on being the same as – and doing the same as – everybody else. We know that all the children we work with, for example, have different skills and abilities, likes and dislikes, hopes and fears, and so on. We need to appreciate those differences and act in a way that shows that we accept those differences, rather than trying to pretend that everybody is the same.

So when it comes to tree-climbing, for example, some children have been told that they are not allowed to climb trees because there is one child whose physical impairment means that tree-climbing is not an option for them at that setting. So everybody is being treated the same – but how fair is that to all the children involved – both the ones who want to climb trees and the child with the physical impairment who could end up with no mates because it's her fault the others can't have their fun? And how does this sort of treatment help children to understand that 'difference' is positive, rather than something which makes everybodys' lives a misery?

By making such blanket rules we are making several assumptions and may therefore end up with a few prejudices – all in the name of anti-discriminatory practice! The child with the physical impairment might not want to climb trees – she might be scared of heights or just not fancy it! (Or she might be able to do it with help but we haven't quite thought about that…)

We have also assumed that children will not be able to respect each other unless adults lay down some conditions in which this can happen.

So the black hole of discrimination can drag us in — even when we think we're doing the right thing.

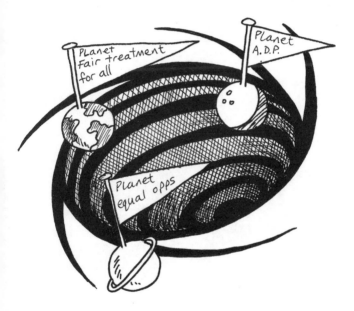

But we need to remember that discrimination is about treating people differently on the basis of prejudice — not just about treating them differently. Some people need different treatment to be treated equally — and that's not the same as treating people the same.

## Escape from the black hole...

So in this chapter we have looked at how, despite all our good adp intentions from Chapter 2, the practice in our settings can create stereotypes, prejudice and discrimination – even when we think we are on the right track. We need to use our adp skills at all times – with ourselves, in our settings and, finally, with other people...

# Chapter 4

You've probably noticed that there is no title for this chapter. That's because I have a small problem with it, and I'd like to share it with you before we go any further. This chapter probably should really be called something like, 'challenging discrimination'. But the trouble with the 'c' word is that, in my experience, it puts most people right off. Remember how we talked about images in our heads in Chapter 1, and how these can give rise to some quite strong feelings? Well, it seems to me that lots of people hear the phrase 'challenging discrimination' and get a mental image of thrusting somebody against a wall menacingly so that they promise not to be such a sexist/homophobe/idiot the next time. Enough to put anybody off challenging discrimination for life really – so you see my problem.

So perhaps we can just pause a minute here whilst I launch a little competition. If, once you're read this chapter, you can come up with a better title for this chapter than 'challenging discrimination', then send it in to the office and we'll send you a free 'Buskers Guide' if we agree with you! (By the way, do feel free to try out your idea in the gap on the contents page and see how it looks first!)

Anyway, enough fun – back to the grindstone… For those of you who are stuck with that mental image of the wall and feeling that you are being required to come over all aggressive, then relax – it's just not going to be like that. We'll get to what it is going to be like in a minute – but first of all, we just need to be sure about our professional role when it comes to talking to other people in terms of adp.

## Pro-active adp

As we said in Chapter 1, discrimination can have a harmful effect on children's development, and therefore it is part of our professional role not only to prevent discrimination in our own practice and in our own settings, but also to be 'anti-discrimination' in our wider work context. So it's simply not enough to shrug our shoulders and say, 'Not me guv – I'm not sexist/racist/homophobic…' and then carry on as if discrimination does not exist. Because even if it was the case that we could all remain perfectly stereotype-prejudice-discrimination-free all day every day (which is a bit of a tall order I think you'll agree!), discrimination affects the lives of all the children and families we work with.

So we have to be pro-active, rather than reactive. Just as many of us have got 'eyes in the backs of our heads' when it comes to children's safety, we also need to develop some invisible antennae which alert us to discrimination and potential discrimination. This doesn't mean, by the way, that we all have to turn into unbearable demagogues of adp — it just means that we can all become more aware of stereotype-prejudice-discrimination and try to do something about it when we come across them.

Anti-discriminatory practice therefore needs to be a regular, everyday part of our professional practice, part of the way that we think and act all the time, rather than something that we only do when somebody prods us into it.

It's also probably worth emphasising here that although we are 'anti-discrimination', we shouldn't restrict ourselves just to taking action when discrimination happens. Because the point about being pro-active is that we are – well, pro-active! – and as we said in Chapter 1, in some situations it may be possible to deal with stereotypes and prejudices before they lead to discrimination. Or maybe taking action could mean that stereotypes and prejudices are not passed on to the children we work with. So instead of waiting for the unfair treatment to take place, we need to counteract stereotypes and prejudices as we come across them.

**Realistic expectations**
When we are discussing stereotypes or prejudices with other people, it is important to remember that all we are aiming to do is to simply put across another point of view, make people aware of other ways of seeing things, highlight false assumptions, supply some missing facts or contribute different experiences to a discussion.

What we are not trying to do is to change peoples' minds or to transform their personal values and attitudes. As we said in Chapter 1, values and attitudes are very often embedded deep within us and in our professional role, it is quite unlikely that we will have the kind of relationship with colleagues, parents or even children that makes very profound personal discussions possible (or even desirable).

So the thing that we are aiming to do in most of our

discussions involving stereotypes and prejudice is to put across a straightforward message about there being another way of seeing things, rather than the transformation of somebody's views – however difficult we may find some of those views. (Some views will of course not be acceptable in the setting and this will need to be dealt with through the setting's policies and procedures, as will any cases of discrimination that cannot be resolved as a result of discussion.)

**Talking the talk**
Conversations about stereotypes and/or prejudices can seem daunting, but as we said earlier, it's really not a case of having to pin people against a wall, or even trying to delve into their deeply-held personal views.

All we need to do is;

- have confidence in our professional values
- be able to put those values across calmly, confidently and assertively
- remember that we are not in a competition to win 'adp of the year' (!)
- using 'I' instead of 'you' to focus on the issue rather than the person
- concentrate on putting across another point of view, rather than getting the person to apologise for their values and attitudes
- keep our tone of voice light – no lectures please!
- vary language and context depending on whether we are talking to children or adults
- appreciate that the other person may have based their views on a significant personal experience
- choose an appropriate time to raise an issue – this is not always straight after something has been said
- avoid putting ourselves in any sort of danger in the name of adp (ok, so maybe I've worked in some really tough places, but it has been known!)
- try to make sure that we part on good terms.

**Walking the walk**
So now, at the end of Chapter 4 and, indeed, the end of this Buskers Guide, we've had our word salad, dodged the black hole of discrimination and put paid to the dragons made out of cardboard boxes once and for all (we really have, haven't we – you're not just humouring me now, are you?!). We've talked the talk and now it's time to get on with walking the walk – so, lead the way!